Alice in Wonderland
A PLAY

ALICE
IN WONDERLAND

A Play

Dodgson, Charles Hodgson

COMPILED FROM LEWIS CARROLL'S STORIES

Alice in Wonderland and *Through the Looking-Glass, and What Alice Found There*

BY

Emily Prime Delafield

Originally presented, for the benefit of The Society of Decorative Art, at The Waldorf, New York, March thirteenth, 1897, and now for the first time printed

---

NEW YORK

DODD, MEAD & COMPANY

1898

PR4611
A72D4
1898

17750

IT MAY be interesting to lovers of "Alice in Wonderland" and "Through the Looking Glass" to know how the thought of compiling a play from those stories suggested itself to me. In 1890, while visiting Japan, I was invited to attend a performance, by children, of scenes from the former book. I went reluctantly, fearing a travesty on familiar characters. I came away delighted with the entertainment, and feeling that until then I had only half understood the cleverness of the book. There were but few English children in Yokohama who could be called upon to act, and the preparations were necessarily very crude. When, therefore, I was asked to suggest something new to be given for the benefit of the Society of Decorative Art, on the anniversary of the opening of the Waldorf, March 14, 1897, I determined to compile this play. As the work went on I found that it would add much to the dramatic effect if I took scenes from both "Alice in Wonderland" and "Through the Looking Glass," and while appreciating fully the difficulty of my task, I believed that the interest aroused by seeing Alice herself and all the other familiar characters in propria persona would more than atone for any shortcomings in my work.

We formed our troupe of about sixty children, varying in ages from four to twelve. The relative sizes for the different characters, as well as the costumes, we copied carefully from Tenniel's illustrations. These accompany all the different editions of the books and can easily be obtained. The birds and animals were made of paper and paper-muslin and canton flannel, which made excellent imitations of feathers and skins. The Mouse was dressed in canton flannel and had a very long tail, which was appropriate to its story. The heads of all the animals and birds were bought at a toy store for a very little money, and were thin and light. The mouths which were closed we cut open, otherwise the voices would have been muffled.

In Act II, where the Walrus and the Carpenter eat the oysters which were run in on wires, the oysters were painted with small human heads coming out of the shells which stood on end and hands thrown up as if protesting.

The tea-party scene in Act IV, where the Dormouse was turned head foremost by the March Hare and Hatter into a very large teapot, brought down the house.

The dance in Act VI, in which all the animals take part who have entered after the song by the Mock Turtle, was very pretty.

*In the last act, instead of the curtain ris-
ing after the royal party and court were
seated, we formed a procession of all the
animals, birds, courtiers and attendants,
which entered after the curtain rose.
They marched round the stage, all those
not taking an active part forming a group
behind the chairs of the King and Queen.
This brought on all the characters of the
play and made a very effective scene.
For the rest, we carried out the stage di-
rections as given. These had been carefully thought out, and have since on two
occasions practically proved to be good.
We taught the children thoroughly their
parts, and left to them the interpretation
of the characters, with, we thought, better results than if we had imposed our
ideals upon them. But of course we chose
our little troupe with care. The children thoroughly enjoyed the rehearsals,
learned how to use their voices and to*

enunciate distinctly, and showed the great-
est cleverness in their acting. We had
every reason to feel pleased at the interest shown by the audience in the play.

EMILY PRIME DELAFIELD.

CHARACTERS

Alice	Frog-Footman
Queen	Gryphon
King	Walrus
Duchess	Carpenter
Knave	Cheshire Cat
Executioner	Two of Spades
Tweedledee	Five of Spades
Tweedledum	Seven of Spades
Humpty Dumpty	Magpie
Hatter	Eagle
Dormouse	Duck
March Hare	Dodo
White Rabbit	Lory
Caterpillar	Jabberwock
Mock Turtle	Knight
Fish-Footman	Crocodile

Mouse

Three Judges
The Queen's Four Children
A Herald
Jurors, Ladies-in-Waiting, &c.

ACTS

ACT FIRST

The Garden—Alice and the Animals—The Mouse's Story

ACT SECOND

Tweedledum and Tweedledee—The Fish-Footman and Frog-Footman—The Cheshire Cat.

ACT THIRD

The Caterpillar and Alice—Humpty Dumpty—The Jabberwock Song.

ACT FOURTH

The Tea Party—March Hare—Hatter—Dormouse.

ACT FIFTH

The Queen's Croquet Party—Procession.

ACT SIXTH

The Gryphon and Mock Turtle—The Lobster Quadrille.

ACT SEVENTH

The Trial.

¶

Who cares for you? You're nothing but a pack of cards.

ALICE
IN WONDERLAND
𝔄 𝔭𝔩𝔞𝔶

ACT I

A GARDEN *Scene. Flowers and wall behind, and hedge in distance through which
there is a hole. Alice asleep under a tree.
White Rabbit hurriedly enters, splendidly dressed,
with fan and gloves in his hands. Large tree at
left, facing stage, in which is a slide where, later
in the play, the Cheshire Cat appears.*

WHITE RABBIT

Oh dear! Oh dear! I shall be too late! [*Alice
wakens; Rabbit looks at watch.*] Oh, my dear
paws! Oh, my fur and whiskers, how late it is
getting: Oh, the Duchess, the Duchess! Won't
she be savage if I have kept her waiting. She'll
get me executed as sure as ferrets are ferrets.

ALICE [*in timid voice*]

If you please, Sir— [*White Rabbit starts and
drops fan and gloves, which Alice picks up. Rabbit disappears through a hole under the hedge seen in
the distance and is followed by Alice. Alice comes*

back out of breath and throws herself down on the bank.] Dear, dear! How queer everything is to-day! And yesterday things went on just as usual. I wonder if I've been changed in the night? Let me think: Was I the same when I got up this morning? I almost think I can remember feeling a little different. But if I'm not the same, the next question is, who in the world am I? Ah, that's the great puzzle! [*Sits down and thinks.*] I wonder if I can remember all the things I used to know. Let me see: four times five is twelve, and four times six is thirteen, and four times seven is—oh dear! I shall never get to twenty at that rate! However, the Multiplication Table don't signify: let's try Geography. London is the capital of Paris, and Paris is the capital of Rome, and Rome—no, *that's* all wrong, I'm certain! I'll try and say "How doth the little"—[*Crosses her hands on her lap and in a hoarse voice says:*]

How doth the little crocodile
Improve his shining tail,
And pour the waters of the Nile
On every golden scale.

[*Enter the Crocodile, who dances before her and opens and shuts his mouth and spreads his claws, while Alice recites the last verse, and backs gradually off the stage.*]

How cheerfully he seems to grin,
How neatly spreads his claws,
And welcomes little fishes in
With gently smiling jaws!

[*Enter the Mouse while Alice recites last verse,
runs in a great hurry across the stage appearing
preoccupied and not noticing Alice.*]

I'm sure those are not the right words. [*Sees the
Mouse.*] I wonder if I could speak to the Mouse;
I suppose mice can talk—things are so queer
down here. [*Aloud, to Mouse.*] Mouse, dear, will
you tell me the way out of here? [*Mouse jumps
when Alice speaks to him, and runs out. Alice begins to cry. Splashing in the water is heard in the
distance.*] Why, it must be a walrus or hippo-
potamus to make such a noise. [*Mouse runs in
again followed, in single file, by Duck, Dodo, Lory,
and an Eaglet and other animals, all wet.*] Dear
me! Here is Noah's ark. Mouse, dear, why
are they all so wet?

M O U S E

Ask these gentlemen.

E A G L E T

Here we are so wet; how are we to get dry?

M O U S E

Sit down, all of you, and listen to me! I'll soon
make you dry enough. [*All sit in a ring, Mouse*

in centre.] Ahem! Are you all ready? This is the driest thing I know. Silence all round.

"William the Conqueror, whose cause was favoured by the pope, was soon submitted to by the English, who wanted leaders, and had been of late much accustomed to usurpation and conquest."

LORY
Ugh!

MOUSE [*politely frowning*]
I beg your pardon! Did you speak?

LORY
I?

MOUSE
I thought you did,—I proceed. "Edwin and Mercer, the earls of Mercia and Northumbria, declared for him; and even Stigand, the patriotic archbishop of Canterbury, found it advisable"—

DUCK
Found *what*—

MOUSE [*crossly*]
Found *it;* of course you know what "it" means.

DUCK
I know what "it" means well enough when I find anything; it's generally a frog or a worm. The question is, what did the archbishop find?

MOUSE

Find? Found it advisable to do just what he wanted to. [*Turning to Alice.*] How are you getting on?

ALICE [*in a melancholy tone*]

You see they are just as wet as ever; it doesn't seem to dry them at all.

DODO

I move the meeting adjourn for the adoption of energetic remedies.

EAGLET

Speak English. I don't know the meaning of half those long words and what's more I don't believe you do either.

Bends down his head to hide a smile. The other birds titter audibly.

DODO

What I was going to say, was, that the best thing to get us dry would be a Caucus-race.

ALICE

What *is* a Caucus-race?

DODO

The best way to explain it is to do it. Are you ready?

Music. Dodo marks out a course; all race and come out alike. All crowd around him and ask:

A L L

Who has won?

Dodo puts finger on his forehead, in the position you usually see Shakespeare, in the pictures of him.

D O D O

Everybody has won, and all must have prizes.

C H O R U S

But who is to give the prizes?

D O D O [*pointing at Alice*]

Why, *she*, of course.

All crowd round Alice, calling, " Prizes ! Prizes !" Alice pulls out box of candies, and hands them round as prizes. There is exactly one apiece, all round.

M O U S E

But she must have a prize herself.

D O D O

Of course. [*To Alice.*] What else have you got in your pocket?

A L I C E

Only a thimble.

D O D O

Hand it over here. [*All crowd round Alice. Dodo solemnly presents the thimble to Alice, saying:*] I beg your acceptance of this elegant thimble.

All cheer. Mouse begins to run away. Alice calls him back.

A L I C E
Mouse! Mouse! You promised to tell me your history. [*Mouse does not return.*]

A L L [*persuasively*]
Do please come back and tell us a story.

A L I C E
I wish I had Dinah here. She'd soon fetch it back.

A L L
Who is Dinah?

A L I C E
Dinah's our cat. And she's such a capital one for catching mice. And, oh, I wish you could see her after the birds! Why, she'll eat a little bird as soon as look at it!

This speech causes a remarkable sensation among the party. Some of the birds hurry off at once; one old Magpie begins wrapping itself up very carefully, remarking:

M A G P I E
I really must be getting home: the night-air doesn't suit my throat. Come away, my dears! It's high time you were all in bed.

On various pretexts they all move off, and Alice is soon left alone.

A L I C E [*half crying*]
I wish I hadn't mentioned Dinah! Nobody seems to like her down here. Mouse, dear, do come back, I won't talk of Dinah any more. *Begins to cry. Mouse returns, followed by all the birds.*

M O U S E
Mine is a long, sad tale.

A L I C E [*looking at Mouse's tail*]
It's a very long one, but why a sad one?

M O U S E
Here is my story:

> Fury said to
>   a mouse, That
>   he met
>   in the
>   house,
>   " Let us
>   both go
>   to law :
>   I will
>   prosecute
> *you.* —
>   Come, I'll
>   take no
>   denial ;
>   We must

have a
trial :
For
really
this
morning
I 've
nothing
to do."
Said the
mouse to
the cur,
"Such a
trial,
dear sir,
With no
jury or
judge
would be
wasting
our breath."
"I 'll be
judge,
I 'll be
jury,"
Said
cunning
old Fury :
"I 'll try

the whole
cause,
and
condemn
you
to
death."

They all go off the stage, two and two, keeping time with their index fingers pointed, while saying from " I 'll try the whole cause." *Alice watches them.*

Curtain falls.

ACT II

DROP *scene in back of the stage. Sea with sand beach and rocks to left on stage. Tweedledum and Tweedledee sidle in under a tree with their arms round each other's neck, and Alice knows which is which, because one has* "DUM" *embroidered on his collar, and the other* "DEE."

ALICE [*examining them*]

I suppose they have "TWEEDLE" on the back of their collar.

Tweedledee and Tweedledum stand very still, when Alice is startled by hearing a voice coming from the one marked "DUM."

TWEEDLEDUM

If you think we're wax-works, you ought to pay, you know. Wax-works weren't made to be looked at for nothing. Nohow!

TWEEDLEDEE

Contrariwise, if you think we're alive, you ought to speak.

ALICE [*apologetically*]

I'm sure I'm very sorry. [*Aside.*] I cannot help thinking of the old song:

"Tweedledum and Tweedledee
   Agreed to have a battle;
For Tweedledum said Tweedledee
   Had spoiled his nice new rattle.

Just then flew down a monstrous crow,
   As black as a tar-barrel;
Which frightened both the heroes so,
   They quite forgot their quarrel."

TWEEDLEDUM

I know what you're thinking about, but it
isn't so, nohow.

TWEEDLEDEE

Contrariwise, if it was so, it might be; and if
it were so, it would be; but as it isn't, it ain't.
That's logic.

ALICE

I was thinking, which is the best way out of
this wood; it's getting so dark. Would you
tell me, please? [*Tweedledum and Tweedledee look
at one another and grin. Alice points her finger at
Tweedledum.*] First Boy!

TWEEDLEDUM [*briskly*]
Nohow!

Shuts his mouth with a snap.

A L I C E [*points at Tweedledee*]
Next Boy!

T W E E D L E D E E
Contrariwise!

T W E E D L E D U M [*pointing at Alice*]
You've begun wrong! The first thing in a visit
is to say "How d'ye do?" and shake hands.
[*Here the two brothers give each other a hug and
then they hold out the two hands that are free, to
shake hands with Alice, who takes hold of both
hands at once. All dance round in a ring; music
plays: "Here we go round the Mulberry bush."
They suddenly leave off dancing. Music stops; they
let go Alice's hands and stand looking at her very
hard. Tweedledum pants, out of breath.*] Four
times round is enough for one dance.

A L I C E
I hope you're not much tired.

T W E E D L E D U M
Nohow. And thank you very much for asking.

T W E E D L E D E E
So much obliged. Do you like poetry?

A L I C E
Yes! Some poetry.

T W E E D L E D U M

Repeat to her "The Walrus and the Carpenter," that's the longest.

Gives his brother an affectionate hug.

T W E E D L E D E E

Let's each read her a verse by turns.

Here Alice interrupts.

A L I C E [*doubtfully*]

If it's very long, would you please tell me first which road—

Tweedledee and Tweedledum only smile and continue without stopping. Enter the Walrus and the Carpenter, who walk slowly round and round. Carpenter has a large basket on his arm in which are a loaf of bread, pepper pot, salt pot and a number of oyster shells, off of which later they are supposed to eat the oysters. While the poem is recited, oysters painted, of different sizes, are run in on a wire across sea and pass out behind rocks, after all being massed on the stage. Four come in at verse VI, four more at verse VIII, four more at first line of verse IX and then four and eight and eight all during verse IX. They are massed on stage and do not go off until part leave at last two lines of verse XVII and then all the rest at verse XVIII.

T W E E D L E D U M
I

The sun was shining on the sea,
Shining with all his might;
He did his very best to make
The billows smooth and bright—
And this was odd, because it was
The middle of the night.

T W E E D L E D E E
II

The moon was shining sulkily,
Because she thought the sun
Had got no business to be there
After the day was done—
"It's very rude of him," she said,
"To come and spoil the fun."

T W E E D L E D U M
III

The sea was wet as wet could be,
The sands were dry as dry.
You could not see a cloud, because
No cloud was in the sky;
No birds were flying overhead—
There were no birds to fly.

T W E E D L E D E E
IV

The Walrus and the Carpenter
Were walking close at hand;

They wept like anything to see
Such quantities of sand;
"If this were only cleared away,"
They said, "it would be grand."

T W E E D L E D U M

v

"If seven maidens with seven mops
Swept it for half a year,
Do you suppose," the Walrus said,
"That they could get it clear?"
"I doubt it," said the Carpenter,
And shed a bitter tear.

T W E E D L E D E E

vi

"O Oysters, come and walk with us," *[Enter four oysters.]*
The Walrus did beseech.
"A pleasant walk, a pleasant talk,
Along the briny beach;
We cannot do with more than four,
To give a hand to each."

T W E E D L E D U M

vii

The eldest Oyster looked at him,
But never a word he said;
The eldest Oyster winked his eye,
And shook his heavy head—
Meaning to say he did not choose
To leave the oyster-bed.

T W E E D L E D E E

VIII

But four young Oysters hurried up, [*Enter four oysters.*]
All eager for the treat;
Their coats were brushed, their faces washed,
Their shoes were clean and neat—
And this was odd, because, you know,
They hadn't any feet.

T W E E D L E D U M

IX

Four other Oysters followed them, [*Enter four oysters.*]
And yet another four; [*Enter four more.*]
And thick and fast they came at last, [*Enter eight.*]
And more, and more, and more— [*Enter eight.*]
All hopping through the frothy waves,
And scrambling to the shore.

T W E E D L E D E E

X

The Walrus and the Carpenter
Walked on a mile or so,
And then they rested on a rock
Conveniently low;
And all the little Oysters stood
And waited in a row.
Walrus and Carpenter sit down.

T W E E D L E D U M

XI

"The time has come," the Walrus said,
"To talk of many things;

Of shoes—and ships—and sealing wax—
Of cabbages—and kings—
And why the sea is boiling hot—
And whether pigs have wings."

T W E E D L E D E E

XII

"But wait a bit," the Oysters cried,
"Before we have our chat;
For some of us are out of breath,
And all of us are fat!"
"No hurry!" said the Carpenter.
They thanked him much for that.

T W E E D L E D U M

XIII

"A loaf of bread," the Walrus said,
"Is what we chiefly need;
Pepper and vinegar besides
Are very good indeed—
Now if you're ready, Oysters dear,
We can begin to feed."

*Carpenter hands Walrus loaf of bread and shows
him one immense pepper pot and one salt pot; the
last two are stood in the rocks between them. Walrus cuts off slice of bread.*

T W E E D L E D E E

XIV

"But not on us!" the Oysters cried,
Turning a little blue.

"After such kindness, that would be
A dismal thing to do!"
"The night is fine," the Walrus said.
"Do you admire the view?

TWEEDLEDUM
xv
"It was so kind of you to come!
And you are very nice!"
The Carpenter said nothing but
"Cut us another slice;
I wish you were not quite so deaf—
I've had to ask you twice!"

TWEEDLEDEE
xvi
"It seems a shame," the Walrus said,
"To play them such a trick,
After we've brought them out so far,
And made them trot so quick!"
The Carpenter said nothing but
"The butter's spread too thick!"

TWEEDLEDUM
xvii
"I weep for you," the Walrus said;
"I deeply sympathize,"
With sobs and tears he sorted out
Those of the largest size,   [*Exit some oysters.*]
Holding his pocket-handkerchief
Before his streaming eyes.

T W E E D L E D E E

XVIII

"O Oysters," said the Carpenter,   [*Exit all the oysters.*]
"You've had a pleasant run!
Shall we be trotting home again?"
But answer came there none—
And this was scarcely odd, because
They'd eaten every one.

A L I C E

I like the Walrus best, because he was a little
sorry for the poor oysters.

T W E E D L E D E E

He ate more than the Carpenter, though. You
see he held his handkerchief in front, so that
the Carpenter couldn't count how many he
took.

A L I C E

That was mean! Then I like the Carpenter
best.

T W E E D L E D E E

But he ate as many as he could get.

A L I C E

Well! They were both very unpleasant characters—[*Here she stops, alarmed at seeing it grow
darker.*] Do you think it is going to rain?

Tweedledum spreads a large carriage umbrella over himself and his brother and looking up from under it, says:

T W E E D L E D U M

No, I don't think it is; at least—not under *here*. Nohow. But it may rain outside.

T W E E D L E D E E

It may—if it chooses, we've no objection. Contrariwise.

A L I C E [*aside*]

Selfish things. I'd better go.

Starts to leave, when Tweedledum springs from under the umbrella and seizes her by the wrist.

T W E E D L E D U M [*pointing to a small thing lying under the tree*]

Do you see that?

A L I C E [*after examining the thing carefully*]

It's only a rattle [*she adds hastily*] not a rattle-snake, you know.

T W E E D L E D U M

I knew it was.

Stamps about and tears his hair; here he looks at Tweedledee, who sits down on the ground and tries to hide himself under the umbrella.

A L I C E [*laying her hand on his arm*]

You needn't be so angry about an old rattle.

T W E E D L E D U M [*very angry*]

But it isn't old! It's new, I tell you — I bought it yesterday. My nice new rattle.

His voice rises to a scream. All this time Tweedle-dee tries his best to fold up the umbrella with him-self in it; he ends by rolling over, bundled up in the umbrella, with his head out; and he lies there opening and shutting his mouth and his large eyes.

A L I C E [*aside, looking at him*]

Well! You look more like a fish than anything else.

T W E E D L E D U M [*to Tweedledee*]

Of course you agree to have a battle.

T W E E D L E D E E [*sulkily*]

Well! I suppose so. [*Crawling quite out of um-brella.*] Only she must help to dress up, you know.

Tweedledum and Tweedledee go off, hand-in-hand, into the wood, and return with their arms full of things, — bolsters, blankets, hearth-rugs, table-cloths, dish-covers and coal-scuttles, prepared so that they can be tied on, and one long wooden sword.

T W E E D L E D U M

I hope you're a good hand at pinning and tying strings; every one of these things has got to go on somehow or other.

Alice dresses them up in all the things until they look like bundles.

ALICE [*aside*]
Really, they look more like bundles of old clothes than anything else. [*Alice arranges a bolster round the neck of Tweedledee, saying, aside,*] This is to keep his head from being cut off.

TWEEDLEDEE [*very gravely*]
You know it's one of the most serious things that can possibly happen in battle to get one's head cut off.

Alice laughs, but manages to turn it into a cough. Tweedledum comes up to have his helmet tied on.

TWEEDLEDUM
Do I look very pale?

ALICE [*in a low tone*]
Well—yes—a little.

TWEEDLEDUM [*in a low voice*]
I'm very brave generally, only to-day I happen to have a headache.

TWEEDLEDEE
And I've got a toothache! I'm far worse than you.

ALICE [*gently*]
Then I wouldn't fight to-day, if I were you.

TWEEDLEDUM

We must have a bit of a fight, but I don't care about going on long. What's the time now?

Tweedledee pulls out big turnip watch.

TWEEDLEDEE [*looking at watch*]

Half-past four.

TWEEDLEDUM

Let's fight till six and then have dinner, and she [*pointing to Alice*] can watch us—only you'd better not come very close; I generally hit everything I can see—when I get really excited.

Whirls round and round with sword stretched out just missing everything.

TWEEDLEDEE

And I hit everything within reach, whether I see it or not.

ALICE [*laughs*]

You must hit the trees pretty often, I should think.

TWEEDLEDUM [*looks round with a satisfied smile*]

I don't suppose there'll be a tree left standing for ever so far round, by the time we've finished.

ALICE

And all about a rattle! I should feel ashamed
to fight about such a trifle.

TWEEDLEDUM

I should not have minded so much, if it hadn't
been a new one. [*To his brother.*] There's only
one sword, you know, but you can have the
umbrella—it's quite as sharp—only we must
begin quickly. It's getting as dark as it can.

ALICE

Why, who is this?

Enter Fish-Footman with very large letter, sealed.
Frog-Footman comes forward from behind the trees,
and takes the note.

FISH

For the Duchess,—where is the Duchess? An
invitation from the Queen to play croquet.

Fish-Footman goes off the stage.

FROG

From the Queen, an invitation to play croquet.

TWEEDLEDUM and TWEEDLE-
DEE [*to one another*]

And we're not asked; what an insult.

Begin to cry; go off the stage followed by Frog-Foot-
man; Alice remains. Head of Cheshire Cat appears
among branches of tree.

A L I C E [*to herself*]
I wonder what became of the baby that turned
into a pig. If it has grown up — [*sees head of
Puss*] Would you tell me, please, which way
I ought to walk from here ?

C A T
That depends a good deal upon where you want
to go to.

A L I C E
I don't much care where.

C A T
Then it doesn't matter which way you walk.

A L I C E
So long as I get somewhere.

C A T
Oh, you're sure to do that if you'll walk long
enough.

A L I C E
What sort of people live about here ?

C A T
In that direction [*pointing to the right*] lives a
Hatter ; and in that direction [*pointing to the left*]
lives a March Hare — visit either you like,
they're both mad.

A L I C E
But I don't want to go among mad people.

CAT

Oh, you can't help that; we're all mad here. I'm mad and you're mad.

ALICE

How do you know I'm mad?

CAT

Why, you must be or you would not have come here.

ALICE

And how do you know that you're mad?

CAT

Why, to begin with, a dog's not mad; you grant that?

ALICE

I suppose so.

CAT

Well, then you see a dog growls when it's angry and wags its tail when it's pleased. Now I growl when I'm pleased, and wag my tail when I'm angry, therefore, I'm mad.

ALICE

I call it *purring*, not growling.

CAT

Call it what you please. Do you play croquet with the Queen to-day?

A L I C E

I should like to very much, but I haven't been invited yet.

C A T

You'll see me there. [*Cat vanishes, by means of slide in tree. Cat reappears.*] By-the-by, what became of the baby?

A L I C E

It turned into a pig.

C A T

I thought it would.

Cat vanishes.

A L I C E

I've seen Hatters before, and a March Hare would be much the most interesting, and perhaps as this is May it won't be raving mad, at least not so mad as it was in March.

C A T [*reappearing*]

Did you say pig, or fig?

A L I C E

I said pig, and I wish you wouldn't keep appearing and vanishing so suddenly; you make me quite giddy.

C A T [*vanishing slowly*]

All right.

ALICE

Well! I've often seen a cat without a grin, but a grin without a cat is the most astonishing thing that I've seen in all my life—what next?

Curtain falls.

ACT III

HUMPTY Dumpty sitting on the wall, which is back and to right of stage, rolling from time to time as if he would roll off. Caterpillar sitting on toad-stool at centre of stage smoking a Hooka. Enter Alice who stands opposite Caterpillar and they look at one another. Mattrass behind the wall for Humpty Dumpty to fall on must not be seen.

CATERPILLAR [*contemptuously*]
You! Who are you?

ALICE [*drawing herself up*]
I think you ought to tell me who you are.

CATERPILLAR
Why? [*Alice turns away crossly.*] Come back! I have something important to say.

ALICE [*aside*]
This sounds promising.

Turns back.

CATERPILLAR
Now! Keep your temper.

ALICE [*gulping as if controlling her anger*]
Is that all?

CATERPILLAR [*puffing away at the pipe*]
So you think you are changed, do you?

ALICE

I'm afraid I am, Sir; I can't remember things
I used to.

CATERPILLAR

Can't remember what things?

ALICE [*melancholy*]

Well, I've tried to say "How doth the little
busy bee," but it is all different.

CATERPILLAR

Repeat "You are old, Father William."

ALICE

"You are old, Father William, the young man
   said,
And your hair has become very white;
And yet you incessantly stand on your head—
Do you think, at your age, it is right?"

CATERPILLAR

That is not said right.

ALICE

Not quite right, I'm afraid.

CATERPILLAR [*decidedly*]

It is wrong from beginning to end.

ALICE [*indignantly*]

I have never been so contradicted in my life;
I am losing my temper.

CATERPILLAR [*curls itself up on toad-stool, pipe in its mouth*]
You ought to be content, then.

Humpty Dumpty sitting on a wall; Alice sees him and goes over and looks at him.

ALICE
Humpty Dumpty himself. It can't be anybody else. I'm as certain of it, as if his name were written all over his face. [*Humpty Dumpty, with immovable face, sitting with his legs crossed, like a Turk.*] How exactly like an egg he is.

HUMPTY DUMPTY
It's *very* provoking, to be called an egg—*very.*

ALICE
I said you looked like an egg, Sir. And some eggs are very pretty, you know.

HUMPTY DUMPTY
Some people have no more sense than a baby.

Alice stands as if not knowing what to do next; finally says softly to herself:

ALICE
"Humpty Dumpty sat on a wall;
Humpty Dumpty had a great fall.
All the King's horses and all the King's men
Couldn't put Humpty Dumpty in his place
    again."

That last line is much too long for the poetry.

H U M P T Y   D U M P T Y

Don't stand chattering to yourself like that, but tell me your name and your business.

A L I C E

My *name* is Alice.

H U M P T Y   D U M P T Y

It's a stupid name enough! What does it mean?

A L I C E [*doubtfully*]

Must a name mean something?

H U M P T Y   D U M P T Y

Of course it must; my name means the shape I am—and a good handsome shape it is, too. With a name like yours, you might be any shape, almost.

A L I C E

Why do you sit out here all alone?

H U M P T Y   D U M P T Y

Why, because there's nobody with me. Did you think I didn't know the answer to *that?* Ask another.

A L I C E

Don't you think you'd be safer down on the ground? That wall is so very narrow.

H U M P T Y   D U M P T Y
What tremendously easy riddles you ask. [*Growls out in low voice.*] Of course I don't think so. Why, if ever I did fall off—which there's no chance of—but if I did—[*here he purses up his lips, and looks so solemn and grand that Alice can hardly help laughing.*] If I did fall, the King has promised me—oh, you may turn pale, if you like. You didn't think I was going to say that, did you? The King has promised me—with his very own mouth—to—to—

A L I C E
To send all his horses and all his men.

H U M P T Y   D U M P T Y
Now I declare that's too bad. You've been listening at doors—and behind trees—and down chimneys—or you couldn't have known it.

A L I C E
I haven't indeed. It's in a book.

H U M P T Y   D U M P T Y
Ah, well! They may write such things in a book. That's what you call a History of England. Now, take a good look at me! I'm one that has spoken to a King, I am; mayhap you'll never see such another; and to show you I'm not proud, you may shake hands with me. [*Smiles from ear to ear and nearly falls off the*

wall in taking Alice's hand.] Yes, all his horses
and all his men. They would pick me up again
in a minute, they would. However, this con-
versation is going on a little too fast; let's go
back to the last remark but one.

A L I C E
I'm afraid I can't quite remember it.

H U M P T Y   D U M P T Y
In that case we start fresh, and it's my turn to
choose a subject.

A L I C E [*aside*]
He talks about it just as if it were a game.

H U M P T Y   D U M P T Y
Well, here's a question for you. How old did
you say you were?

A L I C E [*makes a short calculation on her fingers*]
Seven years and six months.

H U M P T Y   D U M P T Y
Wrong! You never said a word like it.

A L I C E
I thought you meant "How old *are* you?"

H U M P T Y   D U M P T Y
If I'd meant that, I'd have said it. [*Alice does
not reply.*] Seven years and six months. An un-

comfortable sort of age. Now if you'd asked my advice, I'd have said "Leave off at seven" —but it's too late now.

A L I C E
I never ask advice about growing.

H U M P T Y   D U M P T Y
Too proud.

A L I C E [*looking very indignant*]
I mean, that one can't help growing older.

H U M P T Y   D U M P T Y
One can't, perhaps, but two can. With proper assistance you might have left off at seven.

A L I C E
What a beautiful belt you've got on. At least, I mean, a beautiful cravat. I should have said —no, a belt, I mean—I beg your pardon. If only I knew, which was neck and which was waist.

Humpty Dumpty looks very angry, though he says nothing for a minute or two. When he does speak again, it is in a deep growl.

H U M P T Y   D U M P T Y
It's a most—provoking—thing, when a person doesn't know a cravat from a belt.

A L I C E
I know it's very ignorant of me.

HUMPTY DUMPTY

It's a cravat, child, and a beautiful one, as you
say. It's a present from the White King and
Queen. There now!

ALICE

Is it really?

HUMPTY DUMPTY

They gave it to me [*crosses one knee over the other
and clasps his hands round it*] they gave it me—
for an un-birthday present.

ALICE

I beg your pardon.

HUMPTY DUMPTY

I'm not offended.

ALICE

I mean, what is an un-birthday present?

HUMPTY DUMPTY

A present given when it isn't your birthday,
of course.

ALICE [*thinks a little*]
I like birthday presents best.

HUMPTY DUMPTY

You don't know what you are talking about!
How many days are there in a year?

A L I C E
Three hundred and sixty-five.

H U M P T Y   D U M P T Y
And how many birthdays have you?

A L I C E
One.

H U M P T Y   D U M P T Y
And if you take one from three hundred and sixty-five, what remains?

A L I C E
Three hundred and sixty-four, of course.

H U M P T Y   D U M P T Y
That shows that there are three hundred and sixty-four days when you might get un-birthday presents—

A L I C E
Certainly.

H U M P T Y   D U M P T Y
And only one for birthday presents, you know. There's glory for you.

A L I C E
I don't know what you mean by "glory."

H U M P T Y   D U M P T Y [*contemptuously*]
Of course you don't—till I tell you. I meant "there's a nice knock-down argument for you."

A L I C E

But "glory" doesn't mean "a nice knock-down argument."

H U M P T Y   D U M P T Y

When I use a word it means just what I choose it to mean — neither more nor less.

A L I C E [*in a thoughtful tone*]

That's a great deal to make one word mean.

H U M P T Y   D U M P T Y

The question is, which is to be master. That's all. Good-bye.

A L I C E

Good-bye, till we meet again.

H U M P T Y   D U M P T Y

I shouldn't know you again if we did meet [*giving her one of his fingers to shake*]; you're so exactly like other people.

A L I C E [*shakes his finger*]

The face is what one goes by, generally.

H U M P T Y   D U M P T Y

That's just what I complain of. Your face is the same as everybody has — the two eyes, so [*marking their places in the air with his thumb*], nose in the middle, mouth under. It's always the same. But if you had the two eyes on the same side of the nose, for instance—or the mouth at the top—that would be some help.

A L I C E
It wouldn't look nice.

H U M P T Y   D U M P T Y
Wait till you've tried.

Alice waits to see if he will speak again, but as he never opens his eyes or takes any further notice of her, she says " Good-bye ! " once more, and getting no answer to this, runs off to the right, but stops, seeing a book lying on the ground, picks it up and turns over the leaves to find some part she can read but finds none.

A L I C E
It is all in some language I don't know. [*Puzzles over it and then exclaims :*] To be sure, it's a looking-glass book ! I must read it backwards.

C A T E R P I L L A R
Give it to me. You're stupid. [*Reads.*]

I
'Twas brillig, and the slithy toves
Did gyre and gimble in the wabe;
All mimsy were the borogoves,
And the mome raths outgrabe.

[*At end of each verse turns to Alice and explains :*]
Brillig means four o'clock in the morning, you

know. The time when you begin broiling things
for dinner.

*Jabberwock comes in; moves slowly round and
round towards the back of stage, and then goes out
again.*

II

Beware the Jabberwock, my son!
The jaws that bite, the claws that catch!
Beware the Jubjub bird, and shun
The frumious Bandersnatch!

*The Jabberwock suddenly runs in pursued by
Knight. Humpty Dumpty sitting upon a wall.*

III

He took his vorpal sword in hand;
Long time the manxome foe he sought—
So rested he by the Tumtum tree,
And stood a while in thought.

IV

And as in uffish thought he stood,
The Jabberwock, with eyes of flame,
Came whiffling through the tulgey wood,
And burbled as it came!

V

One, two! One, two! And through and through
The vorpal blade went snicker-snack!
He left it dead, and with its head
He went galumphing back.

A L I C E
Explain! Explain!

C A T E R P I L L A R
Well, "slithy" means "lithe and slimy," "lithe" is the same as "active." It's like a portmanteau. There are two meanings packed in one word. But you're too stupid for me [*contemptuously*].

Crash is heard and Humpty Dumpty falls off the wall backwards on a mattrass out of sight behind the wall.

Curtain falls.

ACT IV

GARDEN Scene. *There is a table set under the trees a little to the right, slightly back of stage, with an arm-chair at the end to the left, and four chairs at the side facing the audience, another arm-chair to the right at the end, the table littered with cups and saucers, a pitcher of milk, a big teapot in the middle and bread and butter to left. The March Hare and the Hatter are having tea at the table; the Dormouse is sitting between them fast asleep and the other two are using it as a cushion, resting their elbows on it, and talking over its head. Enter Alice who walks towards the table and says:*

ALICE
Very uncomfortable for the Dormouse, only, as it's asleep, I suppose it doesn't mind.

ALL THREE [*March Hare, Hatter and Dormouse to Alice*]
No room! No room!

ALICE
There's *plenty* of room!

Sits down in a large arm-chair at one end of the table.

MARCH HARE [*in encouraging tone*]
Have some wine?

ALICE
I don't see any wine.

MARCH HARE
There isn't any.

ALICE
Then it wasn't very civil of you to offer it.

MARCH HARE
It wasn't very civil of you to sit down without being invited.

ALICE
I didn't know it was your table; it's laid for a great many more than three.

HATTER
Your hair wants cutting.

He has been looking at Alice for some time with great curiosity, and this is his first speech.

ALICE
You should learn not to make personal remarks. It's very rude.

Hatter opens his eyes very wide on hearing this.

HATTER
Why is a raven like a writing desk?

ALICE [*aside*]
Come, we shall have some fun now! I am glad they have begun asking riddles—[*to Hatter*] I believe I can guess that.

MARCH HARE

Do you mean you think you can find out the answer to it?

ALICE

Exactly so.

MARCH HARE

Then you should say what you mean.

ALICE

I do, at least I mean what I say—that's the same thing, you know.

HATTER

Not the same thing a bit! Why, you might just as well say that I see what I eat is the same thing as I eat what I see.

MARCH HARE

You might just as well say that I like what I get is the same as I get what I like.

DORMOUSE [*who seems to be talking in his sleep*]

You might just as well say that I breathe when I sleep is the same thing as I sleep when I breathe.

HATTER

It *is* the same thing with you. [*All sit silent for a little while.*] What day of the month is it?

Takes his watch out of his pocket and looks at it uneasily, shaking it every now and then, and holding it to his ear.

A L I C E [*thinks a little*]
The fourth.

H A T T E R
Two days wrong! I told you butter wouldn't suit the works!

M A R C H   H A R E
It was the best butter.

H A T T E R
Yes, but some crumbs must have got in as well. You shouldn't have put it in with the bread-knife.

The March Hare takes the watch and looks at it gloomily; then he dips it into his cup of tea, and looks at it again.

M A R C H   H A R E
It was the best butter, you know.

Alice has been looking over the shoulder of March Hare with some curiosity.

A L I C E
What a funny watch! It tells the day of the month and doesn't tell what o'clock it is.

H A T T E R
Why should it? Does your watch tell you what year it is?

ALICE

Of course not, but that's because it stays the same year for such a long time together.

HATTER

Which is just the case with mine.

ALICE [*looks dreadfully puzzled*]

I don't quite understand you.

HATTER

The Dormouse is asleep again.

Pours a little tea on his nose. The Dormouse shakes his head impatiently.

DORMOUSE

Of course, of course; just what I was going to remark myself.

HATTER

Have you guessed the riddle yet?

ALICE

No, I give it up; what's the answer?

HATTER

I haven't the slightest idea.

ALICE

I think you might do something better with the time, than wasting it in asking riddles that have no answers.

HATTER

If you knew Time as well as I do, you wouldn't talk about wasting *it*. It's *him*.

ALICE

I don't know what you mean.

HATTER

Of course you don't! I dare say you never even spoke to Time.

ALICE

Perhaps not, but I know I have to beat time when I learn music.

HATTER

Ah! that accounts for it. He won't stand beating. Now if you only kept on good terms with him, he'd do almost anything you liked with the clock. For instance, suppose it were nine in the morning, just time to begin lessons: you'd only have to whisper a hint to Time, and round goes the clock in a twinkling. Half-past one, time for dinner!

MARCH HARE [*in whisper*]

I only wish it was.

ALICE

That would be grand, certainly, but then—I shouldn't be hungry for it, you know.

HATTER

Not at first, perhaps, but you could keep it to half-past one as long as you liked.

ALICE

Is that the way you manage?

HATTER [*shakes his head mournfully*]

Not I. We quarrelled last March—just before he went mad, you know—[*pointing with his tea-spoon at the March Hare*] it was at the great concert given by the Queen of Hearts, and I had to sing

> "Twinkle, twinkle, little bat!
> How I wonder what you're at!"

ALICE

It goes on, you know, in this way:

> "Up above the world you fly,
>   Like a tea-tray in the sky.
>   Twinkle, twinkle—"

Here the Dormouse shakes himself, and begins singing in his sleep, "Twinkle, twinkle, twinkle, twinkle—" *and goes on so long that they have to pinch him to make him stop.*

HATTER

Well, I'd hardly finished the first verse, when the Queen bawled out "He's murdering the time! Off with his head!"

A L I C E
How dreadfully savage.

H A T T E R
And ever since that, he won't do a thing I ask.
It's always six o'clock now.

A L I C E
Is that the reason so many tea-things are put
out here?

H A T T E R
Yes, that's it; it's always tea-time, and we've
no time to wash the things between whiles.

A L I C E
Then you keep moving round, I suppose?

H A T T E R
Exactly so; as the things get used up.

A L I C E
But when you come to the beginning again?

M A R C H   H A R E
Suppose we change the subject. I'm getting
tired of this. I vote the young lady tells us a
story.

A L I C E [*rather alarmed at the proposal*]
I'm afraid I don't know one.

March Hare and Hatter shake the Dormouse.

A L L

Then the Dormouse shall. Wake up, Dormouse.

Dormouse slowly opens his eyes.

D O R M O U S E

I wasn't asleep, I heard every word you fellows were saying.

M A R C H   H A R E

Tell us a story !

A L I C E

Yes, please do.

H A T T E R

And be quick about it, or you'll be asleep again before you begin.

D O R M O U S E [*beginning in great hurry*]

Once upon a time there were three little sisters ; and their names were Elsie, Lucie and Tillie ; and they lived at the bottom of a well—

A L I C E

What did they live on ?

D O R M O U S E [*after thinking a moment*]

They lived on treacle.

A L I C E

They couldn't have done that, you know : they'd have been ill.

DORMOUSE
So they were, very ill.

Dormouse constantly goes to sleep while telling his story and is shaken up by March Hare and Hatter.

ALICE
Why did they live at the bottom of a well?

MARCH HARE [*very earnestly*]
Take some more tea.

ALICE
I've had nothing yet, so I can't take more.

HATTER
You mean, you can't take *less*; it's very easy to take more than nothing.

ALICE
Nobody asked *your* opinion.

HATTER [*triumphantly*]
Who's making personal remarks now?

Alice does not quite know what to say to this; so she helps herself to some tea and bread and butter, and then turns to the Dormouse, and repeats her question.

ALICE
Why did they live at the bottom of the well?

Dormouse takes a minute or two to think about it.

D O R M O U S E
It was a treacle-well.

A L I C E [*very angrily*]
There's no such thing.

*Hatter and March Hare say "Sh! sh!" and the
Dormouse sulkily says:*

D O R M O U S E
If you can't be civil, you'd better finish the
story for yourself.

A L I C E [*very humbly*]
No, please go on! I won't interrupt again. I
dare say there may be *one*.

D O R M O U S E [*indignantly*]
One, indeed! And so these three little sisters
—they were learning to draw, you know—

A L I C E
What did they draw?

D O R M O U S E
Treacle.

H A T T E R
I want a clean cup, let's all move one place on.

*The Hatter upsets the milk-cup as he moves and the
Dormouse follows him; the March Hare moves into
the Dormouse's place, and Alice rather unwillingly
takes the place of the March Hare. The Hatter is*

*the only one who gets any advantage from the change ;
and Alice is a good deal worse off than before, for
the March Hare has just upset the milk-jug into
his plate.*

A L I C E

But I don't understand. Where did they draw
the treacle from?

H A T T E R

You can draw water out of a water-well; so I
should think you could draw treacle out of a
treacle-well, eh, stupid?

A L I C E

But they were *in* the well.

D O R M O U S E

Of course they were—well in. They were
learning to draw [*yawning and rubbing his eyes,
for he was getting very sleepy*], and they drew all
manner of things—everything that begins with
an M—

A L I C E

Why with an M?

M A R C H   H A R E

Why not?

*Dormouse begins going off into a doze, but, on being
pinched by the Hatter, he wakes up again with a
little shriek, and goes on.*

D O R M O U S E
—that begins with an M, such as mousetraps,
and the moon and memory, and muchness—
you know you say things are "much of a muchness"—did you ever see such a thing as a drawing of a muchness?

A L I C E [*very much confused*]
Really, now you ask me, I don't think—

H A T T E R
Then you shouldn't talk.

*This piece of rudeness is more than Alice can bear;
she gets up in great disgust, and walks off; the Dormouse falls asleep instantly, and neither of the others
takes the least notice of her going, though she looks
back once or twice, half hoping that they will call
after her; the last time she sees them, they are trying to put the Dormouse into the teapot, which stands
in front of him.*

Curtain falls.

A C T   V

A GARDEN. *Enter three gardeners with spades and walk up to a large standard rose-tree, which is full of white roses. They begin to paint them red. Enter Alice, who watches them curiously.*

T W O   O F   S P A D E S
Look out now, Five. Don't go splashing paint over me like that.

F I V E   O F   S P A D E S [*sulkily*]
I couldn't help it. Seven jogged my elbow.

S E V E N   O F   S P A D E S
That's right, Five. Always lay the blame on others.

F I V E
You'd better not talk. I heard the Queen say only yesterday you deserved to be beheaded.

T W O
What for?

S E V E N
That's none of your business, Two.

F I V E
Yes, it *is* his business—and I'll tell him—it was for bringing the cook tulip-roots instead of onions.

S E V E N [*throwing down his brush*]
Well — of all unjust things.

Sees Alice, and suddenly stops. The others look round also, and all of them bow low.

A L I C E [*timidly*]
Would you tell me, please, why you are painting those roses ?

Five and Seven say nothing and look at Two.

T W O [*after slight pause, in a low tone*]
Why, the fact is, you see, Miss, this here ought to have been a *red* rose-tree, and we put a white one in by mistake ; and if the Queen was to find it out, we should all have our heads cut off, you know. So you see, Miss, we're doing our best before she comes to —

F I V E [*who has been looking anxiously across the garden*]
The Queen ! the Queen !

Two, Five and Seven instantly throw themselves flat on their faces round the rose-tree.

A L I C E [*looking round eagerly*]
Yes, there they come. What a number of people ! I wonder whether *I* ought to throw myself on my face, like the three gardeners ! I can't remember if there is such a rule at processions. And besides, what would be the use

of a procession if people had to lie down on their faces, so that they couldn't see it? No, I'll stand here and wait!

Tramp of feet is heard behind scene as of many people passing, also beat of drum, and fife, and blast of trumpet. Enter Queen of Hearts, King of Hearts, Executioner and procession. Procession moves across the stage. Children of the Queen, ladies in waiting, officers of the Court, preceded by four heralds with trumps, all to be dressed like a pack of cards. King and Queen leave the procession and come towards the rose-tree. Executioner in the background with axe.

Q U E E N [*to gardeners*]
Get up! [*Seeing Alice.*] Who are you? What's your name, child?

A L I C E [*politely, somewhat tremulously*]
My name is Alice, so please your Majesty.

Q U E E N
And who are *these?*

A L I C E
How should *I* know? It's no business of *mine.*

Q U E E N [*glares at her and screams*]
Off with her head! Off with her head!

A L I C E
Nonsense! Don't talk rubbish.

K I N G [*timidly to Queen*]
Consider, my dear. She is only a child!

Q U E E N [*pointing to gardeners*]
Turn them over. [*King carefully turns them over,
one by one, with his feet. Two, Five and Seven jump
up and bow to King, Queen and Alice, without stopping.*] Leave that off! You make me giddy.
[*Looks at rose-tree.*] What *have* you been doing
here?

T W O [*going down on one knee, humbly*]
May it please your Majesty, we were trying —

Q U E E N
I see! Off with their heads!

The three gardeners run behind Alice for protection.

A L I C E
You shan't be beheaded.

Q U E E N [*shouting and going off the stage*]
Are their heads off?

E X E C U T I O N E R [*shouting*]
Their heads are gone, if it please your Majesty.

Q U E E N [*nearly off stage, still shouting*]
Can you play croquet, Alice?

A L I C E [*shouting*]
Yes!

QUEEN [*roaring*]

Come on, then! I invite you to my croquet party.

Exeunt Queen, King, Executioner and procession.

ALICE

Oh dear! I don't think I'll follow her—at least, not yet! She's sure to want to cut my head off. What a temper she has, to be sure. Heigho! Why, what is that? [*Looks up and sees the grin of the Cheshire Cat in the tree to left of the stage.*] It's a grin—no, it isn't—yes, it is—why, it's the Cheshire Cat! This is nice! Now I shall have somebody to talk to.

CAT

How are you getting on?

ALICE [*aside*]

I must wait till the eyes appear—oh, here they are! It's no use speaking to it, though, till its ears have come, or at least *one* of them.

CAT [*head appearing sideways, only one ear showing*]

There, that's all you will see of me just now. That's quite enough for to-day. Now, how are you getting on at the croquet party?

ALICE

Well, I haven't been there yet, and, to tell you the truth, I don't much care to go. The Queen quarrels so dreadfully with everybody, that I am quite afraid of her.

CAT

How do you like the Queen?

ALICE

Not at all. She's so extremely—

Enter King hurriedly.

KING [*not seeing head of Cheshire Cat*]

Who *are* you talking to, pray? And why don't you come to play croquet with the Queen? She'll be so angry, she'll have your head off if she finds you here. [*Seeing Cat.*] What *is* that you are talking to?

ALICE

It's a friend of mine—a Cheshire Cat. Allow me to introduce it.

KING

I don't like the look of it at all. However, it may kiss my hand if it likes.

CAT

I'd rather not.

KING [*getting behind Alice*]

Don't be impertinent—and don't look at me like that.

A L I C E
"A cat may look at a king." I've read that in some book, but I don't remember where.

K I N G
Well, it must be removed, that's all I know. [*Enter Queen. To the Queen.*] My dear, I wish you would have this Cat removed. I don't like it.

Q U E E N
Off with his head !

K I N G
I thought you would say so. I'll go and fetch the Executioner myself.

Exit King.

A L I C E
I say, don't you think you had better go home ?

C A T
No, I don't mind. I'll stay where I am, I think. Thank you all the same, though.

Q U E E N [*impatiently, looking in direction where the King went off*]
What a long time they are coming.

Enter King and Executioner.

K I N G
I've run so hard, I'm quite out of breath. Here he is, my dear, here he is ! Pray repeat your commands.

Q U E E N [*pointing to Cat's head*]
Off with his head!

E X E C U T I O N E R
Where is he? I don't see him. In fact, I can't
see anybody.

Q U E E N
Don't you see the Cat, you stupid man?

K I N G
Can't you see him up there, grinning as large
as life?

A L I C E [*aside*]
Poor Cheshire Cat! It's all over with him, I'm
afraid.

E X E C U T I O N E R [*seeing Cat*]
Him!

C A T [*benignly*]
Yes, old fellow, they mean *me*. Look hard at
me, while you're about it.

K I N G
Yes, that Cat.

Q U E E N
Don't you understand English?

E X E C U T I O N E R
Yes, I do! What then?

Q U E E N
You're to chop his head off.

E X E C U T I O N E R
I can't.

Q U E E N
You can't?

K I N G [*faintly*]
He can't.

C A T [*quietly*]
I thought as much.

E X E C U T I O N E R
No, I can't. And what's more, I won't, that's
flat. A likely idea that!

K I N G
What do you mean?

Q U E E N
How dare you?

A L I C E [*aside*]
Oh, I'm so glad.

E X E C U T I O N E R
I mean what I say. I can't. And I'll tell you
why. This is my argument: You can't cut off
a head unless there's a body to cut it from;
that's nature, that is. I've never had such a
thing to do before, and I'm not going to begin
at my time of life.

KING

Well, that may be *your* argument. And a very poor one it is, to my idea. Now you look here —this is my argument—everything that's got a head can be beheaded. So don't talk nonsense, and do your duty.

QUEEN

Argument, indeed! Fiddlesticks! If something isn't done about this preposterous business in less than no time, I'll have everybody executed all round. And that's my argument.

ALICE

Please your Majesty, the Cat belongs to the Duchess, hadn't you better ask her about it?

Cat disappears.

QUEEN [*to King*]

Yes, come. We must have the Duchess brought here at once.

Exeunt. Enter the Duchess who tucks her arm affectionately into Alice's from behind and says, close to her ear, resting her chin on her shoulder:

DUCHESS

You're thinking about something, my dear, and that makes you forget to talk. I can't tell you just now what the moral of that is.

ALICE

Perhaps it hasn't one.

D U C H E S S

Tut, tut, child! Everything's got a moral if only you can find it.

Squeezes herself closer to Alice, who looks uncomfortable.

A L I C E [*timidly*]

I think the Queen's croquet party is going on rather better now.

D U C H E S S

'Tis so, and the moral of that is—"Oh, 'tis love, 'tis love, that makes the world go round."

A L I C E [*aside*]

Somebody said, that it's done by everybody minding their own business.

D U C H E S S

Ah, well. It means much the same thing [*digs her sharp little chin into Alice's shoulder*] and the moral of that is—"Take care of the sense, and the sounds will take care of themselves." [*Enter the Queen. Seeing her the Duchess's voice dies away and she begins to tremble. Alice looks up and sees the Queen, who is frowning like a thunderstorm, with her arms folded. The Duchess speaks in a frightened voice.*] A fine day, your Majesty.

Q U E E N

Now, I give you fair warning [*shouting and stamping on the ground*] that either you or your head must be off! Take your choice. [*Duchess goes off in a hurry. Queen turning to Alice.*] Have you seen the Mock Turtle yet?

ALICE

No, I don't even know what a Mock Turtle is.

QUEEN

It's the thing Mock Turtle Soup is made from.

ALICE

I never heard of one.   .

QUEEN

Come on, then, and he shall tell you his history. [*Turns to go out. Enter the Gryphon, who lies down at one side of the stage and goes to sleep.*] Up, lazy thing, and take this young lady to see the Mock Turtle. I must go back and see after some executions I have ordered.

Curtain falls.

DROP *sea scene back of stage. Trees in front left and right of stage. Rocks to left and right on stage with open space between leading down to the water. Gryphon sitting up on rocks to left rubbing its eyes and chuckling; Alice standing by. Mock Turtle on the rocks to the right weeping.*

GRYPHON
What fun!

ALICE
What is the fun?

GRYPHON
Why the Queen. It's all her fancy, that; they never execute nobody, you know. Come on! [*They walk up to the Mock Turtle who looks at them with large eyes filled with tears, but says nothing. Gryphon to Turtle.*] This here young lady, she wants to know your history, she do.

MOCK TURTLE [*in a deep, hollow tone*]
I'll tell it her; sit down both of you, and don't speak a word till I have finished.

No one speaks for a moment or two.

ALICE [*aside*]
I don't see how he can *ever* finish if he doesn't begin.

Waits patiently.

M O C K   T U R T L E [*with a deep sigh*]
Once I was a real Turtle.

Silence for a moment.

G R Y P H O N [*occasionally*]
Hjckrrh!

Mock Turtle sobs and sobs. Alice begins to get up and says:

A L I C E
Thank you, Sir, for your interesting story.

Sits down again as if she thinks there is more to come.

M O C K   T U R T L E [*still sobbing*]
We went to school in the sea. The master was an old Turtle—we used to call him Tortoise—

A L I C E
Why did you call him Tortoise, if he wasn't one?

M O C K   T U R T L E [*angrily*]
We called him Tortoise because he taught us; really you are very dull.

G R Y P H O N
You ought to be ashamed of yourself for asking such a simple question. [*They both sit and look at Alice, who looks as if she would like to sink into the ground. Gryphon to Mock Turtle.*] Drive on, old fellow! Don't be all day about it.

M O C K   T U R T L E

Yes, we went to school in the sea, though you may n't believe it—

A L I C E

I never said I did n't!

M O C K   T U R T L E

You did. [*Mock Turtle goes on with his story.*] We had the best of educations—in fact, we went to school every day.

A L I C E

I've been to a day-school, too; you need n't be so proud as all that.

M O C K   T U R T L E [*anxiously*]

With extras?

A L I C E

Yes, we learned French and music.

M O C K   T U R T L E

And washing?

A L I C E [*indignantly*]

Certainly not!

M O C K   T U R T L E [*in a tone of great relief*]

Ah! Then yours was n't really a good school. Now at *ours* they had at the end of the bill, "French, music, and washing—extras."

A L I C E

You could not have wanted it much, living at the bottom of the sea.

M O C K   T U R T L E [*with a sigh*]

I couldn't afford to learn it. I only took the regular course.

A L I C E

What was that?

M O C K   T U R T L E

Reeling and Writhing, of course, to begin with ; and then the different branches of Arithmetic — Ambition, Distraction, Uglification and Derision.

A L I C E

I never heard of " Uglification." What is it?

The Gryphon lifts up both its paws with surprise.

G R Y P H O N

Never heard of uglifying ! You know what to beautify is, I suppose?

A L I C E [*doubtfully*]

It means — to — make anything — prettier.

G R Y P H O N

Well then, if you don't know what to uglify is, you *are* a simpleton.

A L I C E [*turns to Mock Turtle*]
What else had you to learn?

M O C K   T U R T L E
That's enough about lessons — let's talk of games now. You may not have lived under the sea.

A L I C E
I haven't.

M O C K   T U R T L E
Perhaps you were never even introduced to a lobster —

A L I C E
I once tasted [*stops confused, continues hastily*] no, never.

M O C K   T U R T L E
So you have no idea what a delightful thing a Lobster-Quadrille is.

A L I C E
No, indeed. What sort of a dance is it?

G R Y P H O N
You first form into a line along the seashore —

M O C K   T U R T L E
Two lines. Seals, turtles, salmon, and so on; then, when you've cleared all the jelly-fish out of the way —

GRYPHON [*interrupting*]
That generally takes some time.

MOCK TURTLE [*continuing*]
—you advance twice—

GRYPHON
Each with a lobster as a partner.

Makes a motion of dancing forward as if he had a lobster by the claw.

MOCK TURTLE
Of course ; advance twice, set to partners—

Mock Turtle and Gryphon move back and forward as if in the figure of a quadrille.

GRYPHON
Change lobsters and retire in same order.

MOCK TURTLE
Then, you know, you throw the—

GRYPHON [*interrupting*]
Lobsters ! [*With a shout and bound into the air.*]

Gryphon and Mock Turtle make motions as if throwing imaginary partners out to sea.

MOCK TURTLE
—as far out to sea as you can—

GRYPHON [*with a scream*]
Swim after them.

Both rush towards the sea as if about to plunge in. Mock Turtle makes believe turn a somersault, and capers wildly about.

M O C K   T U R T L E
Turn a somersault in the sea.

G R Y P H O N [*at the top of his voice*]
Change lobsters again.

They move back from sea and towards one another, as if about to go through ladies' chain.

M O C K   T U R T L E
Back to land again, and—[*drops his voice suddenly*] that's the first figure.

The two creatures, who have been jumping about like mad things during this description, sit down quietly and sadly and look at Alice.

A L I C E
It must be a very pretty dance.

M O C K   T U R T L E [*to Gryphon*]
Come, let's try the first figure. We can do it without lobsters, you know. Which shall sing?

G R Y P H O N
Oh, *you* sing. I've forgotten the words.

All the animals and birds come in while the Gryphon is speaking and form in a circle behind Alice, the Gryphon and Mock Turtle. After each verse they bend forward with their right hand to their ear and sing in chorus "Will you, won't you, won't you join the dance." At the end of the second verse they all join in dancing the lobster quadrille to music of song, which continues for quadrille. After which they stand back while Mock Turtle sings "Beautiful Soup," and at the end form a tableau.

M O C K   T U R T L E

"Will you walk a little faster," said a whiting
    to a snail,
"There's a porpoise close behind us, and he's
    treading on my tail,
See how eagerly the lobsters and the turtles all
    advance !
They are waiting on the shingle—will you
    come and join the dance ?
Will you, won't you, will you, won't you, will
    you join the dance ?
Will you, won't you, will you, won't you, won't
    you join the dance ?

"You can really have no notion how delightful
    it will be
When they take us up and throw us, with the
    lobsters, out to sea !"

But the snail replied, "Too far, too far!" and
   gave a look askance—
Said he thanked the whiting kindly, but he
   would not join the dance,
Would not, could not, would not, could not,
   would not join the dance.
Would not, could not, would not, could not,
   could not join the dance.

A L I C E [*in rather a frightened tone*]

Thank you, it's a very interesting dance to
watch, and I like the song about the whiting.

G R Y P H O N

No accounting for tastes! Sing her "Turtle
Soup," will you, old fellow?

M O C K   T U R T L E [*sighing deeply and chok-
ing with sobs, sings*]

  "Beautiful Soup, so rich and green,
  Waiting in a hot tureen!
  Who for such dainties would not stoop?
  Soup of the evening, beautiful Soup!
  Soup of the evening, beautiful Soup!
    Beau-ootiful Soo-oop!
    Beau-ootiful Soo-oop!
  Soo-oop of the e-e-evening,
    Beautiful, beautiful Soup!

Beautiful Soup ! Who cares for fish,
Game, or any other dish ?
Who would not give all else for two
Pennyworth only of beautiful Soup ?
Pennyworth of beautiful Soup ?
   Beau-ootiful Soup !
   Beau-ootiful Soup !
Soo-oop of the e-e-evening,
   Beautiful, beauti-FUL SOUP !"

Tableau.

Curtain falls.

A C T   V I I

ING *and Queen on throne. Fish-Footman
and Frog-Footman on either side at foot of
the throne. Gentlemen in Waiting and Ladies
in Waiting on either side. Children of King and
Queen on either side. All the Court massed behind
the throne dressed as cards. On the left, a table for
the three judges, who sit behind raised on a platform.
On the right jury box, with twelve Jurymen. At
the foot of the throne stands the Knave in chains
with a Soldier on either side. Near the King is the
White Rabbit with a trumpet in one hand and a
scroll of parchment in the other. In the middle of the
court is a table with a large dish of tarts upon
it. The King who acts as head judge wears his
crown on top of a big white wig. All the other judges
wear wigs. The twelve jurors each have a slate
and are the animals and birds who have been characters in the play. Present are Gryphon, Mock
Turtle, Humpty Dumpty, The Duchess, Hatter,
March Hare, Dormouse, etc.*

KING

Herald, read the accusation!

*White Rabbit blows three blasts on the trumpet;
then he unrolls the parchment and reads as follows:*

WHITE RABBIT

"The Queen of Hearts, she made some tarts,
All on a summer day;
The Knave of Hearts, he stole those tarts,
And took them quite away!"

KING [*to jury*]
Consider your verdict.

WHITE RABBIT
Not yet, not yet! There's a great deal to come before that!

KING
Call the first witness.

Rabbit blows three blasts on the trumpet and calls out:

WHITE RABBIT
First witness!

The first witness is the Hatter, who comes with a teacup in one hand and a piece of bread and butter in the other.

HATTER
I beg your pardon, your Majesty, for bringing these in; but I hadn't quite finished my tea when I was sent for.

KING
You ought to have finished. When did you begin?

Hatter looks at the March Hare, who has followed him into court, arm in arm with the Dormouse.

H A T T E R
Fourteenth of March, I think it was.

M A R C H   H A R E
Fifteenth.

D O R M O U S E
Sixteenth.

K I N G [*to jury*]
Write that down. [*Jury write down all these dates on their slates.*] Take off your hat.

H A T T E R
It isn't mine.

K I N G [*to jury*]
Stolen !

Jury instantly make a memorandum of the fact.

H A T T E R
I keep them all to sell. I 've none of my own. I 'm a hatter.

Here the Queen puts on her spectacles and begins to stare hard at the Hatter who fidgets.

K I N G
Give your evidence ; and don't be nervous, or I 'll have you executed on the spot.

Hatter keeps shifting from one foot to the other, looks uneasily at the Queen and in his confusion bites a large piece out of his teacup instead of the bread and butter. Dormouse crosses the court and Queen says to officer:

QUEEN [*to officer*]

Bring me the list of singers in the last court concert.

KING

Give your evidence, or I'll have you executed, whether you're nervous or not.

HATTER

I'm a poor man, your Majesty, and I hadn't but just begun my tea—not above a week or so—and what with the bread and butter getting so thin—and the twinkling of the tea—

KING

The twinkling of *what?*

HATTER

It *began* with the tea.

KING

Of course twinkling begins with a T! Do you take me for a dunce? Go on!

HATTER

After that I cut some more bread and butter—

ONE OF JURY
But what did the Dormouse say?

HATTER
That I can't remember.

KING
You *must* remember, or I'll have you executed.

Hatter drops his teacup and bread and butter and falls on his knees.

HATTER
I'm a poor man, your Majesty.

KING
You're a very poor speaker. If that's all you know about it, you may stand down.

HATTER
I can't go no lower. I'm on the floor, as it is.

KING
Then you may sit down, or leave the court-room. [*Hatter hurriedly leaves court.*] Call the next witness.

WHITE RABBIT
Alice!

ALICE
Here!

K I N G

The trial cannot proceed until all the Jurymen
take their places. What do you know of this
business ?

A L I C E

Nothing.

K I N G

Nothing whatever ?

A L I C E

Nothing whatever.

K I N G

That's very important.

W H I T E   R A B B I T

Unimportant, your Majesty means.

K I N G

Unimportant, of course, I meant. Silence !
[*Reads from his book.*] Rule Forty-two.

**All persons more than a mile high to leave the
court.**

A L I C E

I'm not a mile high.

K I N G

You are.

QUEEN
Nearly two miles.

ALICE
Well, I shan't go, at any rate; besides, that's
not a regular rule; you invented it just now.

KING
It's the oldest rule in the book.

ALICE
Then it ought to be Number One.

KING
Consider your verdict.

White Rabbit jumps up in a hurry.

WHITE RABBIT
There's more evidence to come yet, please your
Majesty. This paper has just been picked up.

QUEEN
What's in it?

WHITE RABBIT
I haven't opened it yet, but it seems to be a
letter, written by the prisoner to—to somebody.

JURYMEN
Who is it directed to?

WHITE RABBIT
It isn't directed at all; in fact, there's nothing
written on the *outside*. [*Unfolds paper and says:*]
It isn't a letter after all; it's a set of verses.

JURYMEN
Are they in the prisoner's handwriting?

WHITE RABBIT
No, they're not.

Jury all look puzzled.

KING
He must have imitated somebody else's hand.

Jury all brighten up again.

KNAVE
Please your Majesty, I didn't write it, and they can't prove that I did; there's no name signed at the end.

KING
That only makes the matter worse. You *must* have meant some mischief, or else you'd have signed your name like an honest man.

General clapping.

QUEEN
That *proves* his guilt.

ALICE
It proves nothing of the sort. Why, you don't even know what they're about.

KING
Read them.

WHITE RABBIT

"They told me you had been to her,
And mentioned me to him;
She gave me a good chara&ter,
But said I could not swim.

He sent them word I had not gone
(We know it to be true);
If she should push the matter on,
What would become of you?

I gave her one, they gave him two,
You gave us three or more;
They all returned from him to you,
Though they were mine before.

If I or she should chance to be
Involved in this affair,
He trusts to you to set them free,
Exa&tly as we were.

My notion was that you had been
(Before she had this fit)
An obstacle that came between
Him, and ourselves, and it.

.Don't let him know she liked them best,
For this must ever be
A secret, kept from all the rest,
Between yourself and me."

KING

That's the most important piece of evidence we've heard yet ; so let the jury —

A L I C E

If any of them can explain it, I'll give him six-pence. *I* don't believe there's an atom of meaning in it.

Jury all write down on their slates, but none of them attempt to explain.

K I N G [*spreading out verses on his lap*]

If there's no meaning in it, that saves a world of trouble, as we need n't try to find any. And yet I don't know ;
        "—said I could not swim —"
You can't swim, can you ? [*turning to Knave.*]

K N A V E [*sadly*]

Do I look like it ?

K I N G

All right, so far — [*muttering*]
        "We've known it to be true —
        I gave her one, they gave him two —"
Why, that must be what he did with the tarts, you know —

A L I C E

But it goes on, "they all returned from him to you."

K I N G

Why, there they are ! [*Pointing to tarts.*] Nothing can be clearer than that. Then again —
      "—before she had this fit—"
[*to Queen*] you never had fits, my dear, I think ?

Q U E E N [*furiously*]

Never !

K I N G

Then the words don't *fit* you. [*Looks round court
with a smile. There is a dead silence.*] It's a pun !
Let the jury consider their verdict !

Q U E E N

No, no ! Sentence first — verdict afterwards.

A L I C E

Stuff and nonsense ! The idea of having the
sentence first !

Q U E E N

Hold your tongue !

A L I C E

I won't !

Q U E E N [*shouting at top of her voice*]

Off with her head !

Nobody moves.

ALICE

Who cares for you ? You're nothing but a pack
of cards.

A shower of playing cards falls from above.

Curtain falls.

Printed by D. B. Updike
The Merrymount Press
Boston
1898

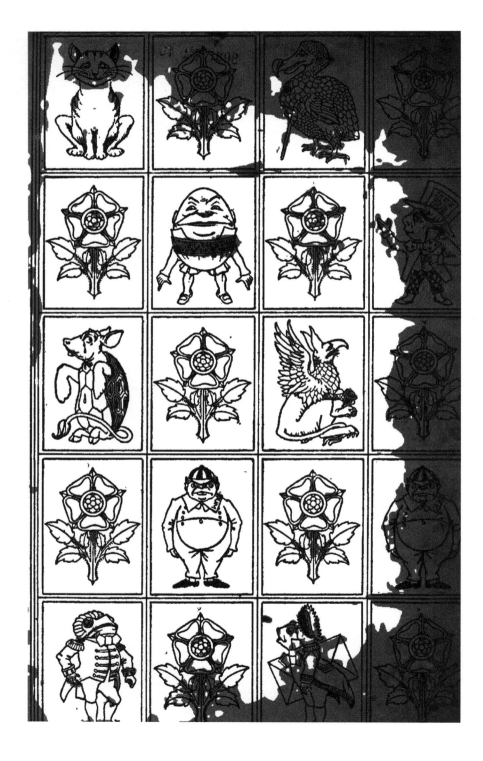

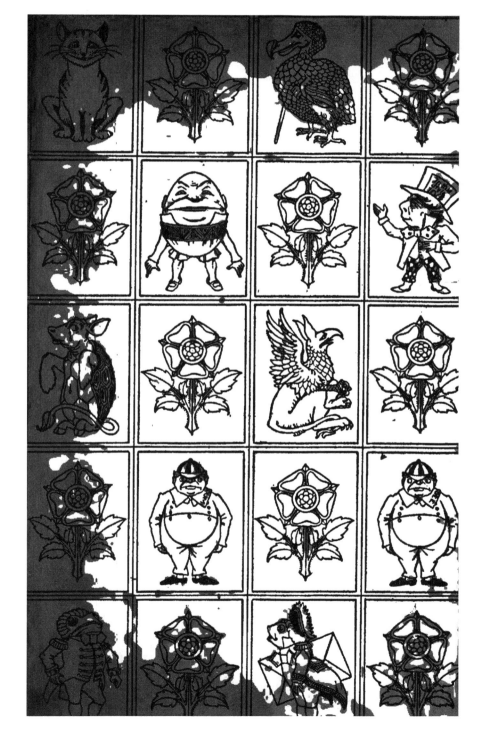

Lightning Source UK Ltd.
Milton Keynes UK
UKHW020220280519
343433UK00004B/195/P